New Zealand
Forest Wildlife

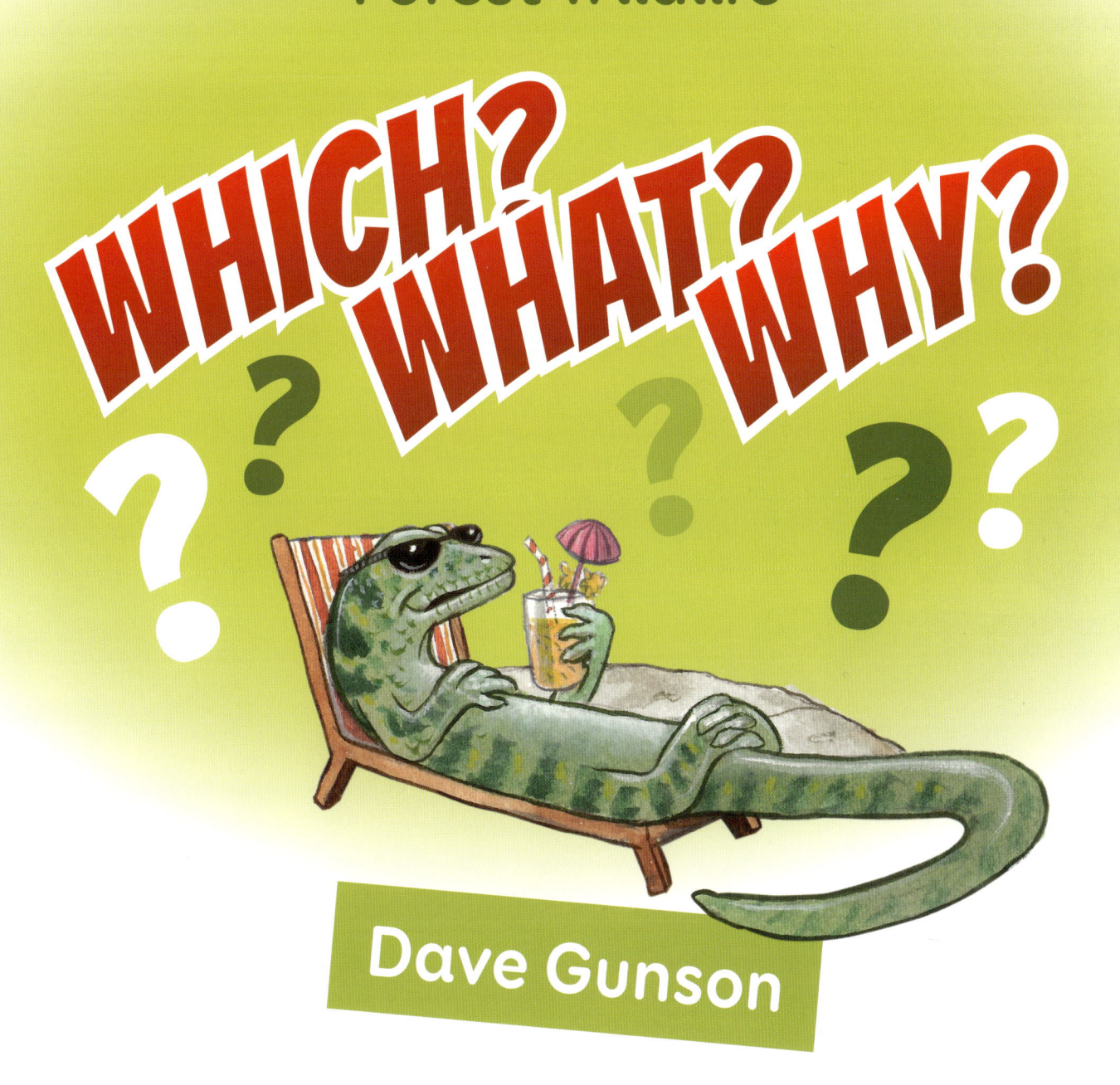

WHICH? WHAT? WHY?

Dave Gunson

BATEMAN BOOKS

How many trees does it take to make a forest?

Oh dear, that's a tricky one! Even though there are hundreds of definitions of the word, it seems that to earn the title of 'forest' the trees need to be close enough together so that they form a cover (leaving a minimal amount of sky that you can see between the tops of the trees). If the trees are more widely spaced, it might be called a 'park' or 'woodland'. It would probably take between 5000 and 10,000 trees for an area to be called a true forest . . . though here in Aotearoa New Zealand we often call a small forest simply 'bush'.

1,012... 1,013... 1,014... 1,015... 1,016...

GEORGE, TEA'S READY!

OKAY, DEAR JUST COMING!

...ER... ...UM...

ONE, TWO, THREE, FOUR ...FIVE...

Are there different sorts of forests in New Zealand, and which one is the biggest?

There are kauri forests in the north of the North Island, which are not forests of kauri trees, but simply forests which have a great number of kauri trees in them. In the South Island and parts of the North Island there are forests where beech trees dominate, and these can be quite 'open' in nature. But the majority of our forests are dense and 'mixed', with many different tree species, depending on the nature of the land, including tōtara, miro, rimu and many others. New Zealand has a great number of large forests of different kinds, and many are contained within forest parks.

The largest forest in New Zealand is the Kāingaroa Forest of planted pine. It covers 2900 square kilometres, and stetches from Kawerau to Lake Taupō.

Are kauri the biggest trees?

Yes, and no. They're certainly the biggest in terms of overall bulk, but not the tallest. Many rimu and tōtara can equal, or exceed, the kauri, and the kahikatea is the tallest of all — at 60 metres or more in height. The trunks of these trees get thinner as they rise, but the trunk of the kauri stays the same width all the way up, and sometimes gets even wider. The greatest kauri tree standing today — the 2000-year-old Tāne Mahuta — measures about 50 metres in height.

The greatest kauri tree ever officially measured was a supergiant called Kairaru, which was about twice the bulk and height of Tāne Mahuta and was probably about 4000 years old when it was lost to a forest fire in the late 1800s.

HOORAY! I WIN!

The largest forest in the world is the Amazon Forest, which is about 5.5 million square kilometres in size — that's more than 20 times the size of New Zealand. Qatar and Greenland don't have any forests at all; in fact, neither place has a single naturally growing tree!

Do kauri snails eat kauri leaves?

No, they don't. They're called kauri snails because they're often found in kauri forests, but not close to kauri trees. They prefer the damp and grassy parts of the forest floor, where they can hide during the day and then come out at night to find insects, grubs and slugs to eat. They will even grab and eat up smaller snails, and they're strong enough to climb some distance up a tree trunk to find their dinner. The snail's 'tongue' is covered in about 10,000 very tiny teeth, to help it devour its prey. The snail's favourite food is worms, and a kauri snail can grab and suck up an earthworm just as fast as a human can suck up a strand of spaghetti!

Kauri snails' shells can measure up to 7.5 centimetres across, and they can live for about 20 years.

HEY, GEROFF! I SAW IT FIRST!

NO, YOU DIDN'T!

DID!

DIDN'T!

DID!

The forests are full of snails of all kinds. There are plenty of large snails and hundreds of small ones. They can be long, short, flat, ridged, smooth, hairy and in all sort of colours. Some are so tiny that they're no wider than a thread of cotton, and they could be passed through the eye of a sewing needle!

Are tree ferns trees or ferns?

They're a bit of both, really. They're a bit like ferns that have evolved to resemble trees. Like 'proper' trees, they have trunks which can suck up the nutrients they need from the roots. They have larger fronds than ordinary ground ferns, and as the tree fern grows upwards, the older fronds drop away as new ones develop and grow. There are 10 species of tree ferns around New Zealand, and the tallest of all is the mamaku, or black tree fern. Unlike other tree ferns, circular scars are left behind on the mamaku's trunk as its 5-metre-long fronds fall away. It can reach 20 metres in height and can live for about 60 years.

The most famous tree fern is the silver fern, or ponga. This tree fern can grow to 10 metres in height and can live for about 60 years. As older fronds fall away from the trunk, just the bases of their stalks are left behind — as a sort of tree fern version of a protective 'bark'. The underside of a frond is silvery-white — earning the name 'silver fern', and it has become a popular symbol of New Zealand.

I'M THE BIGGEST! YAH-BOO, SUCKS TO BE YOU!

THAT'S NOT VERY NICE.

NO, IT ISN'T.

OH, WHO CARES?

COR! THAT'S A CORKER KORU!

How many types of fern are there?

Oh, lots . . . perhaps about 200 species. They range from tiny ferns just 20 millimetres in height, to the 20-metre mamaku. Ferns are a very widespread plant form, with about 20,000 species known around the world; while 40 per cent of New Zealand's ferns are found nowhere else in the world. The coiled frond of a fern is called a koru, and it has become a significant symbol in Māori art, and in New Zealand culture.

Is there something living in the 'cobwebby' holes in the trunks of trees and tree ferns?

Yes, those holes are the homes of tunnelweb spiders. They'll occupy crevices between and under stones, and in holes in trees — and line them, and the openings, with silk. The spider waits inside for a passing insect or slater to touch or disturb the silky 'doorstep' and then will rush out to capture it.

The black tunnelweb spider is the largest of about 25 species of these spiders in New Zealand, and is tough enough to grab a garden snail. It can attack with large, downward-facing fangs and hang on tight, and prevent the snail from withdrawing into its shell. A bite from these spiders can be painful, but is not dangerous.

Most spiders live for about 1 to 3 years, but tunnelwebs can live for about 10 years or more.

AHA! IT MUST BE DINNER TIME!

Are there other holes with spiders inside?

Yes, there are trapdoor spiders, who make holes in the ground to live in, lined with silk. Most trapdoor spiders are found in open country, and mostly in the South Island, and their burrows have a hinged, silken 'lid'. Forest trapdoor spiders don't usually construct a lid for their burrows, and — like the tunnelweb spider — will charge out to capture any insect that passes too close to the burrow entrance.

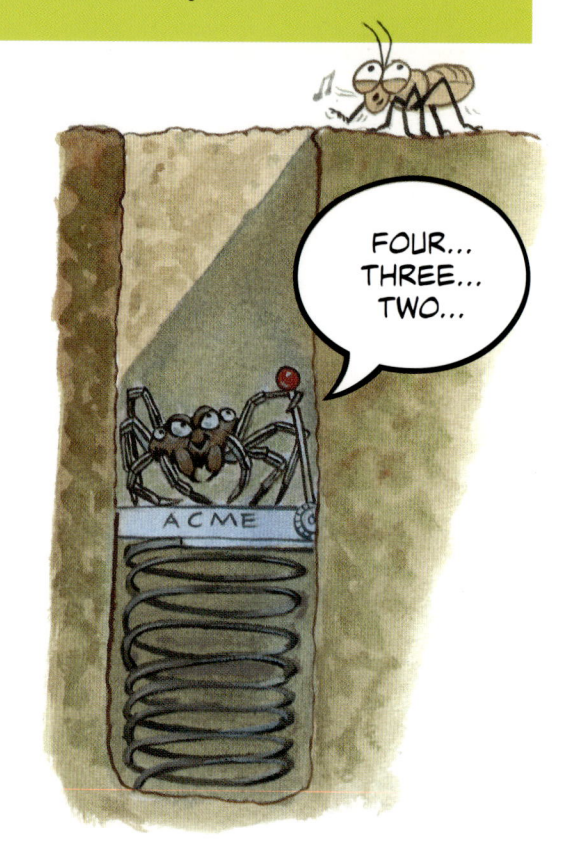

FOUR... THREE... TWO...

Can you make tea from tea-trees?

Yes. Captain Cook's crew first made a slightly bitter tea drink from the leaves. It's more properly called mānuka, and a fine honey is made by bees that visit the mānuka flowers. It forms a tree that is smallish to average-sized, between 4 and 12 metres in height, and it can live for about 60 years.

It's found throughout the country, and in all types of situations: in forests, open country and even high in the mountains. There are several varieties — with flowers ranging from white through to deep pink. Besides honey, the tea-tree has many benefits — seeds, leaves and bark can all be used to treat a variety of ailments. The oils found in the leaves are sometimes used by parakeets to rid themselves of small insect parasites. Many insects, including bees, beetles, flies and moths — and even geckos — find the nectar from the sweet-smelling flowers very attractive.

TEA...*TEA?* AIN'T YOU FELLERS GOT NO *CAWFEE?*

A close relative of tea-tree, or mānuka, is the kānuka — its flowers are only half the size of the mānuka, but it grows to twice the height. And it has many of the health benefits of its smaller cousin.

Are nīkau really palm trees?

Yes, they are. The nīkau is our only native palm tree. They are distant relatives of the more tropical coconut palm trees, and they're the most southerly-growing of all palm trees — even growing far down into the South Island.

They're slow to develop — the young nīkau takes many years to develop a sturdy trunk, and it takes about 30 years before it flowers for the first time. A year or so after flowering, lots of red berries appear — and kererū and kākā love to eat them.

Nīkau can grow to 10 metres or more in height, and can live for more than 100 years.

Millions of years ago — when New Zealand was a much warmer place — there were also coconut palms growing here. But they weren't the very tall palms that can be seen around the Pacific region today, and their coconuts were only about 4 centimetres long — about the size of large walnuts! As temperatures cooled, the coconut palm failed and eventually disappeared, but the nīkau managed to survive.

HEY! STOP SPITTING THE PIPS!

Can bats see in the dark?

No, they can't. They have good eyesight and can see perfectly in daylight, and equally well in low-light conditions — at dusk or dawn. But they can't see in the full dark of night. When flying and hunting for food such as moths and flies, the bat can find them by a sort of echolocation — making sounds which reflect off their prey and receiving the 'echo' with their large ears. Unlike bats overseas, New Zealand bats prefer to forage about on the forest floor, hunting out beetles and other insects.

The New Zealand short-tailed bat is quite small, with a body not much larger than a human's thumb, and weighs only about 16 grams. It can live for about 6 to 10 years.

DAVE DOESN'T KNOW ANYTHING!... OF COURSE WE CAN SEE IN THE DARK!

Bats are the only mammals to have developed true flight — with wings of skin stretched between long finger-bones. There are around 1100 species known around the world, and bats account for 25 per cent of all mammal species.

Bats are some of the fastest flyers. In fact, the fastest mammal in the world is not a cheetah or leopard, but a species of Mexican bat, which can reach speeds of 160 kilometres an hour.

The largest bat in the world is the South Pacific 'flying fox' which can have a wingspan of 1.8 metres, and the smallest is Thailand's 'bumblebee' bat, with a body the size of an adult's thumbnail.

The collective term for bats is a 'colony' or a 'cloud' . . . but Mrs Gunson prefers a **fright** of bats.

What's the strangest animal in the forest?

That has to be the peripatus, also known as velvet worms because of the soft nature of their skin. These tiny creatures — just 2 to 10 centimetres in length — are unique. They are a sort of missing link in the animal kingdom; they look like caterpillars, have segmented bodies like worms do, and have clawed legs like many insects. They're a very ancient kind of animal, going back nearly 500 million years. They live in the damp leaf litter of forests and come out at night to feed on small insects and spiders. They shoot out sticky fluid from glands by their mouths to capture their prey, and then bite and inject a digestive saliva which turns the prey's insides into a 'gloop' which the peripatus can then suck out. There are about 30 species of peripatus in New Zealand, in a wide range of colours, and about 200 known worldwide. They can live for about 5 years.

STRANGE? I'M NOT STRANGE!

YOU ARE A BIT WEIRD THOUGH, ALBERT.

New Zealand's leaf-veined slugs — named for the leaf-like markings on their bodies, of course — are also unusual animals.

Similar species can be found around the South Pacific, but all of New Zealand's 30 or so species are endemic — which means that they are unique to these islands and not found anywhere else. They are usually about 4 to 8 centimetres in length, and appear in a variety of colours — brown, orange, rusty-red, green, grey and so on.

They usually emerge from hiding during the evening to graze on the surfaces of leaves or rotting wood in damp forests, to scrape off the tiny fungi and algal films (very tiny plant growths).

WELL, HELLO THERE, HANDSOME.

HAVE YOU FORGOTTEN YOUR GLASSES AGAIN, BELINDA?

What's the difference between geckos and skinks?

Well, their names are spelt differently, for a start.

Geckos and skinks are both lizards, but there are a lot of differences. Geckos have loose, bumpy, scaly skin, and skinks have much smoother skin, with smaller scales. The eyelids of geckos are fixed in place, which means that they cannot blink, so they have to clean their eyes with a flick of their tongues, while skinks can blink 'properly'.

There are about 40 species of gecko in New Zealand, and while most species around the world lay eggs, our geckos give birth to live young.

Both types of lizard mostly feed on fruits, insects and spiders. Geckos range in size from 8 to 16 centimetres, measured from nose to tail tip, and some can live for up to 40 years. Skinks are usually a bit smaller and sleeker in appearance.

> EEEWWW... WHAT *HAVE* YOU BEEN EATING?

There are about 50 species of skink in New Zealand, and all but one species give birth to live young.

Geckos often have brightly coloured inner mouths. There's a whole range of colours. The forest gecko's tongue and mouth is often orange and yellow, while Gray's tree gecko has a deep blue mouth with a bright red tongue. The Canterbury jewelled gecko may have a pink or mauve mouth, with a pink or orange tongue, and the Otago jewelled gecko has a dark blue mouth, with a black tongue.

Do lizards go to sleep?

Yes, they do. Green geckos are mostly active during the day, and they rest at night. Grey-brown geckos usually prefer to snooze somewhere quiet during the day and then venture out in the evenings to hunt for food.

Most skinks prefer open country, rather than forests, where they can nap under cover, or come out to bask motionless in the sun.

Among all the different types of lizards, only geckos can produce a range of vocal sounds — their name comes from an Asian species call of *gek-oh*. In some places, geckos are called 'chit-chat lizards'. Our own Gray's tree gecko will 'bark' sharply if disturbed.

WHAT'RE YOU UP TO, ROBBO?

SUNBATHING, MATE!

Geckos and skinks can both shed their tails to escape from predators. The tail will twitch and wriggle to distract the attacker while the lizard dashes for safety. It takes a while, but the lizard can then grow a new tail, which is often slightly smaller than the original.

The collective term for lizards is a 'lounge' . . . but Mrs Gunson prefers a **slither** of lizards.

Is the tuatara a lizard?

No, but it's a very special and unique type of reptile. There are only four kinds of reptile: crocodiles and alligators; lizards and snakes; turtles and tortoises . . . and all by itself in the fourth group is the tuatara. There's nothing like it anywhere in the world.

It's a very ancient animal and has remained almost unchanged since the time of the dinosaurs. Tuatara were once widespread through New Zealand, but they are now mostly confined to offshore islands. They live in burrows — sometimes shared with a nesting seabird — and roam about in the evening to feed on skinks, geckos, wētā and beetles. Although a tuatara's teeth are small, its bite is fierce and strong; it has an extra row of teeth in the roof of its mouth, so that the teeth in the lower jaw interlock with the two rows in the upper jaw — making short work of any prey.

OOOH... ALL FOR ME? HOW *LOVELY!*

The name tuatara means 'spiny back' or 'peaks on the back' because of its ridge of soft spines.

Older male tuatara can measure about 60 centimetres from tip to tail, and may live for 60 to 100 years, or longer.

HAPPY 100th TOOTY

There's actually a second species of tuatara — called Gunther's tuatara, which is very similar in size and habits to the more common species. While there are many thousands of the common species, there are only a few hundred Gunther's tuatara surviving in the wild.

Are glow-worms just worms that can glow?

No, they're not. A glow-worm is actually the larva (caterpillar), 20 to 40 millimetres long, of a small fly, which looks very similar to a mosquito. The fly only lives for a few days, and in that time looks for a nice dark place to lay its eggs, such as under a secluded rock overhang, or the ceiling of a cave. Once the larva has hatched and finds a crevice in the rock, it makes a silky sleeve to live in.

HAVE YOU LOST WEIGHT, DEAR?

WELL, I CERTAINLY FEEL LIGHT-ER! HAHA!

THIS BOOK HAS TOO MANY SILLY PUNS...

OH, LIGHTEN UP.

HEY... WHAT'S GOING ON DOWN THERE?

IT'S ANNABELLE'S BIRTHDAY PARTY!

About 70 long, fine lines — 5 to 40 centimetres long — covered in sticky droplets, hang down from the sleeve. The larva has a special organ at the end of its body, which emits light. Flying insects, such as midges and small moths, are attracted to the light, and then get stuck on the lines. The larva can then pull up the line and eat its lunch! If disturbed by a loud noise, the larva will retreat quickly into the rock crevice to conceal the light.

The Waitomo Caves in New Zealand's North Island are generally acknowledged as one of the very best places in the world to see glow-worms. The 30-million-year-old limestone caves are home for many hundreds of thousands of these little self-illuminating larvae.

Do other animals live in caves besides glow-worms?

Yes, there are lots of other small animals — insects and such — that live in forest caves and other dark places. Perhaps the most well-known is the cave wētā.

Although it has a smaller body than the tree wētā — the species that we most regularly see — its very long legs and even longer antennae give it an impressive measurement; one specimen had a measured body length of just 2.5 centimetres, but an overall length of 35 centimetres from its rear feet to the tips of its antennae! And to beat that, there is even a species of *giant* cave wētā that measures up to 45 centimetres by this method — that's 3 centimetres more than the width of the two opened pages of this book that you're holding!

Cave wētā often cluster together in large numbers on cave walls, or upside down on the ceilings. They mostly feed on decaying or fresh plant material, fungi and small insects . . . and sometimes will eat other cave wētā!

WHAT'S ALL THAT STUFF YOU'RE WEARING?

IT'S MY NEW CAVING GEAR!

The long legs of the wētā are not just for show — some can cover over 3 metres in one jump.

Cave wētā make up the largest wētā grouping in New Zealand — there are over 50 species, and perhaps another 500 species known from around the world.

NEARLY WETA TIME... OH WAIT... I'M ON THE WRONG PAGE!... OH BUM!

Another animal that prefers to live in caves is the cave spider. New Zealand has three species, and the largest is the Nelson cave spider . . . found in caves around the Nelson region (well, it would be, wouldn't it?). Its leg span is about 13 to 15 centimetres.

It waits high up on the cave ceilings, and then drops down onto a cave wētā passing below. The first two pairs of legs have long claws, to easily secure its victim. It then retreats up its silken thread, clutching its struggling catch.

The spider's eggs are hung in a ball from the ceiling, and when they hatch, the 80 or more spiderlings will prey on each other until only the last few strongest ones are left.

Spiders are a very ancient form of life — older even than insects. They go back nearly 400 million years in the fossil record. New Zealand has between 2000 and 2500 species, and there are about 75,000 species around the world.

The collective terms for spiders are a 'cluster' or a 'clutter' . . . but Mrs Gunson prefers an **alarm** of spiders.

ARE YOU ONE OF THOSE BIRD-DROPPING SPIDERS?

WELL... I AM NOW!

There are plenty of other spiders in the forests, too. Some of the largest hide in holes in the ground (see page 6). Others spin webs, or hunt through the leaf litter. Others just wait patiently — disguised as parts of flowers, or even looking like bird droppings — for prey to come within grabbing distance.

What's the most dangerous animal in the forest?

There aren't any really dangerous forest creatures in New Zealand. Some insects might give you a nasty bite if you mess with them. And so will some spiders. But the 25-centimetre-long giant centipede is one creature that really shouldn't be disturbed. It has very tough jaws and a venomous bite — more painful than a wasp sting. It moves fast and can easily climb up tree trunks to seek out prey. It's big enough to hunt and attack prey, such as worms, spiders, insects and even skinks and geckos. Some larger centipedes around the world can even catch and eat frogs and mice.

AW, *STINK!*

Centipedes have appeared in the fossil record for about 400 million years, making them a very successful type of animal. There are about 35 species in New Zealand, mostly quite small and secretive, and about 3000 known around the world. 'Centipede' means 100 legs, but they never actually have that many. They might have hundreds of legs, or as few as 14, but never 100.

The long-legged house centipede, 3 centimetres long, shouldn't be regarded as an unwelcome visitor if found in homes around the Auckland area. It will seek out and catch the less desirable intruders — like flies, cockroaches and other insects. It's a sort of natural pest control.

Which is New Zealand's biggest flying insect?

That's the pūriri moth — the largest of all our flying insects, with a wingspan of up to 15 centimetres. The large caterpillars bore holes in the trunks of trees (the pūriri tree is a favourite, obviously) and live in burrows for about seven years, feeding on the inner bark. The adult moths live for only a few days, just enough time to mate and for the female to lay her eggs in the forest's leaf litter — up to 2000 of them. The adult moths have no mouthparts and don't eat during this time. Pūriri moths are found only in the North Island.

WHAT? TWO THOUSAND EGGS, AND I DON'T EVEN GET A TEA-BREAK? GEEZ...

So how big is the giant dragonfly?

It's number two on the list, with a spread of about 13 centimetres. It's also known as the devil's darning needle, which sounds a bit dangerous — but it's really quite harmless. All dragonflies are strong flyers, and some can reach speeds of up to 60 kilometres an hour. They can operate their wings individually, so they can stop, start, go up or down, hover and even fly backwards if they want to!

The giant dragonfly is usually seen around forest waterways, catching insects in flight — its Māori name is kapokapowai, which means 'water snatcher'.

New Zealand has about 11 dragonfly species, and there are up to 6000 species around the world.

THAT'S A 'FAIL'... TRY AGAIN.

DRAGONFLY ADVANCED FLYING SCHOOL

Are insects 'proper' animals?

Yes, they are. The world of living things is divided into groups called kingdoms. Only three can be seen without using a microscope: fungi (mushrooms and the like), plants and animals. So anything that you can see that isn't a fungi or a plant *has* to be an animal . . . from a mosquito to a blue whale, and everything in between, even including me and you!

There are more insects than any other kind of animal — about 900,000 are known, and this accounts for 80 per cent of *all* animal species! Scientists reckon that there could be anything between 2 and 30 million insect species still to be identified, and they estimate that about 80 per cent of the world's insects live in jungles.

Do insects fart?

Probably most of them do, yes. All animals eat and digest food of some sort. As the food is broken down in the gut, a gas is produced which needs to be expelled. Some insects may release this through the fine breathing holes (spiracles) in the sides of their bodies, but most expel gas through the anus (just like humans). Some insects trapped and preserved in amber (fossilised tree resin) millions of years ago show bubbles at the anus — obviously where a gas of some sort has just been released . . . fossil farts!

It's reckoned that the total number of individual insects alive in the world at any one time is about 10 quintillion — that's 10,000,000,000,000,000,000. Or think of it this way — for every person in the world, there are 1500 million insects!

"YOU SHOULD LAY OFF THE CORN, PAL. YOU JUST LOOK SILLY!"

Do any insects have teeth?

No, not like we do. But they do have a lot of different types of mouthparts. Many have sharp and jagged jaws, moving from side to side (our jaws move up and down) that can trap and cut their food — animal or plant — and have structures similar to tongues to help to 'chew' and break down the food into smaller 'swallowable' pieces. Some insects — like mosquitoes — have sharp, hollow 'needles' to pierce the skin of animals or plants to suck out blood or fluids.

Butterflies and most moths have a special mouthpart called a proboscis. This is like a coiled tube that the insect can straighten and use as a sort of straw to suck up liquids like flower nectar, water or juices from soft fruits. Many butterflies actually have taste glands in their feet, so that when they land on a good source of food, the proboscis automatically starts to uncoil — getting ready to suck and swallow!

"GOSH... I DIDN'T KNOW WE COULD DO *THAT*!"

"RECKON WE COULD GIVE IT A TRY, THOUGH..."

"WE CAN'T! DAVE JUST MADE IT UP FOR THIS CARTOON."

How many types of beetle are there in New Zealand?

There are more than 4500 species of beetle in New Zealand, with thousands more still to be identified. That's more than all the numbers of our plant, fish, bird, amphibian, reptile and mammal species *combined*.

The most massive and heaviest is the 5-centimetre-long huhu beetle, but the longest is the giraffe beetle, which can measure up to 9 centimetres in length. And New Zealand's stone beetles are just half a millimetre long.

Huhu beetle grubs can live for two or three years, hidden in old tree trunks and rotten wood in the forests, but the adult beetle only lives for about 20 days. It's a strong and very noisy flyer and can inflict a nasty bite with its sharp jaws.

The grubs of the giraffe beetle also live in old rotten wood, for about 2 years. The adult beetles will sometimes fight — using their long noses as weapons. The smaller female beetle has a shorter snout, and her antennae are set further back, so that she can use it to bore into rotten wood to lay her eggs.

I'M THE BIGGEST!

WELL, I'M THE LONGEST!!

AW, YOU GUYS ARE ALWAYS SHOWING OFF!

The collective terms for beetles are a 'colony' or a 'swarm' . . . but Mrs Gunson prefers a **scuttle** of beetles.

There are more kinds of beetle than any other insect — over 350,000 species have been identified around the world. They make up 40 per cent of all insects, and 30 per cent of all animal species. They can range in size from the 17-centimetre-long Titan beetle from the Amazon rainforest to beetles that are smaller than the full stop at the end of this sentence.

Why are cicadas so LOUD?

It's all the fault of the male cicadas. They drum against special body chambers or clap their wings against a hard surface to make the noise. It's all to attract a female cicada to mate (the females make hardly any noise at all).

When there are lots of cicadas about, it can sound like a deafening hailstorm. Some experts reckon that the noise they make is deliberately loud enough to deter possible bird predators. The female lays eggs in tree bark, and the resulting nymphs drop to the ground, and can spend many years below the surface, feeding on plant roots. When they emerge, they anchor themselves to the bark. Then the skin splits open and the new adult climbs out, leaving the brown empty nymph case attached to the tree.

And then the noise starts again. The aptly named chorus cicada is the most common species in New Zealand, and the adults usually appear sometime in the new year.

There are about 40 cicada species in New Zealand, and they can be found in all environments — the coast, open country, forests and in alpine regions. There are about 3000 species known around the world.

The loudest cicada is a large African species, at 160 decibels — that's louder than a small helicopter passing just 30 metres overhead.

The collective terms for cicadas are a 'cloud' or a 'plague' ... but Mrs Gunson prefers a **din** of cicadas.

Is the kererū really just a big pigeon?

Yes, it is. It has been known as the wood pigeon, or the New Zealand pigeon, but nowadays its more commonly called by its Māori names: kererū, or sometimes kūkū — which is closer to its call of *coo-coo*.

It's a large bird at about 51 centimetres in length and weighing around 650 grams. It sometimes looks like a fat, ungainly bird when sitting on a branch, but in flight it can look quite sleek and streamlined — although it's rather a noisy flyer.

It prefers forest life, but in any town suburb close to areas of native bush, it can often be seen taking a perch on telephone lines for a few moments on its travels.

They're the only bird capable of eating the large fruits of trees such as miro, pūriri, karaka and many others — and then distributing the seeds through their droppings — so the birds are essential for these trees' survival and renewal.

HEY, GET THIS... DAVE RECKONS WE LOOK FAT!

THAT'S NOT VERY NICE!

WE SHOULD ALL GO OVER TO HIS PLACE AND POOP ON HIS CAR!

The collective terms for pigeons are a 'band', a 'kit', a 'flight', a 'dropping', a 'loft', a 'passel', a 'school' or a 'plague' . . . but Mrs Gunson prefers a **coo** of pigeons.

Kererū will often gorge themselves on a variety of large fruits, and then sit in the sun for long periods to digest the food. The trouble is that the flesh of ripe fruits can ferment in the birds' guts and become alcoholic — the kererū get drunk, unbalanced and then fall out of the trees!

Are there any ducks in the forests?

Yes. The blue duck. Its Māori name is whio – after the male's whistling call of *whee-oh* (whio also means 'whistle' in Māori, so that makes sense, doesn't it?). The female duck mostly just says *craak*. This duck prefers to live around the fast-flowing rivers and streams of forests in higher regions. It eats water insects and their larvae by scraping them off the river rocks. The point of its bill is protected from the hard rock by a tip of soft, black skin.

A pair of blue ducks will claim and aggressively defend a stretch of stream or river up to a kilometre in length, and they will chase any intruder away — even an inquisitive kiwi. Chicks are born with extra-large feet, so that they can learn to cope quickly with the fast waters of mountain forest streams.

GOSH... YOU'RE LOOKING VERY BLUE TODAY, COLIN.

YEAH... THE WATER'S FREEZING!

Blue ducks measure about 53 centimetres in length, and if they can avoid predators, such as stoats and wild dogs and cats, they can live for about 13 years.

Do kiwi have wings?

It doesn't look like the kiwi has any wings, but it does have very small ones, hidden under all those feathers. They're not much more than little feather-less wings, with a single claw. The kiwi often tucks its long bill under the wing when it curls up to go to sleep.

Why do kiwi have such long bills?

So they can probe and dig about in the forest undergrowth for things to eat, like grubs, insects and worms. The kiwi's nostrils are located right at the end of its bill, to help it sniff out any tasty morsels. The kiwi also uses its bill and strong legs to fight off any attack — by a predator, or by another kiwi that has strayed into its territory.

I DON'T LIKE GETTING SOIL UP MY NOSE WHEN I'M DIGGING FOR MY DINNER!

Where do kiwi make their nests?

Kiwi nest in burrows under the ground. They often use the weaker soils around tree roots and banks to dig out a short and narrow tunnel, with a nesting area at the back. The female lays her egg (or eggs — the brown kiwi can sometimes lay two) here, and about a week or so after hatching, the chicks are able to explore outside for short periods. They'll stay in their parents' area for a few months before venturing further and finding their own territory.

OH, ISN'T THAT CUTE, KEVIN? HE'S GOT YOUR FEET!

How big is the kiwi's egg?

Very big. It can weigh up to one-fifth of the kiwi's total body weight — that's the highest proportion of any bird in the world. A kiwi egg is equal to about six hen's eggs and can weigh around 450 grams.

Why does the fantail have a tail like a fan?

When the fantail's tail is spread out, it acts like a combination of a rudder and an airbrake, so that the bird can change direction very quickly while it's flying. The fantail can swoop, dive and flutter as it catches flying insects, and it can hover briefly to snatch insects and spiders from leaves and branches. It will also take small fruit from trees. Some birds will even enter houses during summer months to chase and catch flies . . . and then take a quick shower under a garden water sprinkler. Fantails can be seen all around the country, and some all-black forms can be found in southern regions. They can measure about 16 centimetres in length — with the tail accounting for half of that. They can live for about 3 to 10 years.

Which bird is New Zealand's smallest?

The rifleman is our smallest bird. It measures just 8 centimetres from the tip of its bill to the end of its tail. It only weighs about 6 to 7 grams, which is about the same as a $1 coin. It finds food — mostly insects, grubs and spiders — by climbing and hopping up tree trunks in the forest, going around and around upwards as though climbing a spiral staircase.

It's called the rifleman because of its resemblance to the green jackets of early rifle regiments. The Māori name of titipounamu comes from the bird's green plumage — similar to pounamu (greenstone).

LET'S FACE IT BERTIE... YOU NEED TO GO BACK ON YOUR DIET!

How many parrots are there in New Zealand?

Quite a few. There's the 46-centimetre-long kea, which lives in the South Island's alpine zones — no other parrot in the world lives at such high altitudes. It's one of the most intelligent (and inquisitive) birds in the world in the way it can solve difficult and complex puzzles. It's named for its call of *kee-aa*, and can live for about 15–20 years.

The kākā could be regarded as the most 'normal' of our larger parrots, because it flies and climbs through forest trees to seek out beetles, grubs and fruits to eat, just as many parrot species overseas do. Its name comes partly from its call of *kaa*, and the fact that kākā is Māori for 'parrot.' Kākā measure about 45 centimetres in length, and can live for about 20 years.

The smaller parakeets are all green birds, with different-coloured head patches or 'crowns'. Their Māori name is kakariki — meaning 'green' and also 'small parrot'. They call *kita-kita-kita* as they move around in small flocks. They prefer to nest and feed high up in forest trees, feeding on fruits, seeds and leaves. They measure around 24 centimetres and can live for about 5–7 years.

And then there is the heaviest parrot in the world — the kākāpō (see page 28).

The brightly coloured eastern rosella, 33 centimetres long — from Australia — has become established here, and can often be seen in small flocks flying through bush and forest. These birds will eat insects, but they much prefer plant food, especially thistles. They live for about 10 years.

It's estimated that there are about 350 parrot species around the world. The largest flying parrot is the hyacinth macaw from South America. It can measure up to 1 metre in length and weighs up to 1.7 kilograms. The smallest is the pygmy parrot of New Guinea, which measures just a bit over 8 centimetres from tip to tail.

Is the kākāpō *really* a parrot?

Yes, it really is, and it's a record-breaker. It's the only parrot in the world that doesn't fly, and it's also the heaviest parrot in the world, at over 3 kilograms in weight — about twice the weight of the world's largest flying parrot. Like many parrot species, they live a long time by bird standards — up to about 30 to 50 years.

Its name means 'night parrot' because of its habit of staying hidden during the day, and then coming out in the evening to hunt around on the forest floor for young plant shoots and leaves, roots, seeds and fruits. Only rarely will a kākāpō eat insects and grubs.

Its big parrot feet are great for climbing and clambering up tree trunks and branches (and holding out its wings for balance) to reach berries and such. And rather than the hard work of scrabbling and sliding back down the tree again, the kākāpō will often try to jump and then glide back down to the ground.

However, as the females are lighter than the males, they seem to make a much better job of landing safely on the forest floor.

COME ON, PAL. DON'T BE NERVOUS.

WHAT'S HIS PROBLEM?

FIRST-TIME FLYER, I RECKON.

Kākāpō were once widespread through the country, and numbered many thousands, but introduced predators have taken a heavy toll. Kākāpō were given legal protection in 1896, and they are now found in the wild only on predator-free offshore islands.

Can our parrots talk, like those overseas?

They'll mumble, screech, squawk, cry, moan, whistle and cough and even cry like a baby . . . and make lots of other sounds too, but they don't imitate human speech very well — the kākā can make a poor effort at it, and the parakeets were taught a few words by Māori and early European settlers.

Myna are quite capable of copying human speech, though, and can also imitate lots of human-made sounds such as car alarms, bells, whistles, mobile phones and doorbells.

The best bird talker in New Zealand is the tūī. Its natural song is full of coughs, chuckles, whistles, notes, trills and clicks, and it can imitate sounds just like the myna. And it can copy human speech, too. Tūī can be taught to say just about anything that a human can say, and repeat tunes and songs. Māori often taught caged tūī to 'speak' and even to recite a welcome for visitors coming onto a marae!

> HOW ABOUT A SONG THEN? A TUNE? SOMETHING? *ANYTHING?* POLLY WANNA CRACKER?

The collective terms for parrots are a 'prattle', a 'company' or a 'pandemonium' . . . but Mrs Gunson prefers a **chatter** of parrots.

So how do birds 'sing'?

It's all to do with the voice box (in humans, it's called a larynx) — the part of the throat that helps to create the sounds that we make. It stays open when we breathe and closes when we swallow food. When we force air through the larynx, it makes the vocal cords vibrate, which produces sound. We can shape that sound using the parts of the mouth — lips, teeth and tongue.

Although birds have a rigid bill, and don't have a flexible mouth as we do, they do have a special advantage: alone of all animals, nearly all birds have a *double* voice box, called a syrinx.

Some birds have just one set of muscles to control the syrinx, but most songbirds have five to seven sets of muscles to create and control the sounds that they make. They can also produce more than one set of sounds or tunes at a time, and all while breathing in *and* breathing out — trills, warbles, grunts, whistles, chirps, coughs and chirrups . . . *that's* talented birdsong!

I WILL NOW SING GOD DEFEND NEW ZEALAND AND POKAREKARE ANA AT THE SAME TIME, WHILE RIDING A UNICYCLE AND JUGGLING BERRIES!

OH, WE'VE SEEN ALL THIS BEFORE...

YEAH... IT'S JUST STANDARD STUFF.

LAST YEAR WAS BETTER...

The loudest birdsong in the world is that of the Brazilian white bellbird. It can belt out its mating call at over 125 decibels — that's as loud as standing next to a chainsaw, without wearing ear protection!

The longest birdsong belongs to the brown thrasher of North America — it can sing over 2000 different songs.

Is the morepork the only owl in New Zealand?

No, there are a few more. The morepork — or ruru — is by far the most common. But there's also the introduced little owl, which prefers to hunt in daytime in open country rather than night-time in forests, and the barn owl, which has started to establish itself here in small numbers.

Like many owls, the morepork is a 'stealth' hunter. Its wings have soft feathers that enable it to fly down to take prey without making hardly any noise at all.

This — combined with a super hearing ability — make it a very efficient hunter.

The morepork was one of the few birds to benefit from the arrival of human settlers, and their accompanying mice, rats and dogs. The rats and mice preyed on the eggs and chicks from the ground nests of the now-extinct laughing owl (the morepork's predator — and twice its size), and in turn, the same mice and rats gave the morepork a greater range of prey — in addition to settler-introduced small birds, such as the chaffinch.

The morepork will also hunt for ground and flying insects, geckos and skinks.

IT'S TIME FOR BED!

BUT I'VE ONLY JUST GOT UP!

Moreporks are about 29 centimetres long, weigh around 175 grams, and can live for 6 to 10 years. The little owl weighs about the same, is slightly smaller at 23 centimetres, and has a similar lifespan.

The barn owl (also sometimes known as the 'death owl' overseas, because of its screeching call) can measure up to 40 centimetres and weighs about 400 to 600 grams. Its lifespan is often much shorter than the other owls, though.

Text © Dave Gunson, 2021
Typographical design © David Bateman Ltd, 2021

Published in 2021 by David Bateman Ltd
Unit 2/5 Workspace Drive, Hobsonville, Auckland 0618, New Zealand
www.batemanbooks.co.nz

ISBN 978-1-98-853887-7

This book is copyright. Except for the purpose of fair review, no part may be stored or transmitted in any form or by any means, electronic or mechanical, including recording or storage in any information retrieval systems, without permission in writing from the publisher. No reproduction may be made, whether by photocopying or by any other means, unless a licence has been obtained from the publisher or its agent.

The author asserts his moral right to be identified as author of this work.

Illustrations: Dave Gunson
Book design: Alice Bell and Dave Gunson
Printed in China by Toppan Leefung Printing Ltd